Table Of Contents

Chapter 1: Understanding Tax Deductions for Uber Drivers

Overview of Tax Deductions for Uber Drivers

As an Uber, Lyft, or limousine driver, understanding tax deductions is crucial to maximizing your earnings and reducing your tax liability. This subchapter provides an overview of the various tax deductions available to you as a rideshare driver, helping you make informed decisions and optimize your tax return.

One of the key areas where you can maximize tax deductions is rideshare expenses. This includes expenses related to maintaining and operating your vehicle for business purposes. From gas and oil changes to tires and repairs, you can deduct these costs to offset your taxable income.

Additionally, insurance and licensing fees are deductible expenses for Uber drivers. Whether it's liability insurance, commercial auto insurance, or your annual licensing fee, these costs can be claimed on your tax return, reducing your overall tax burden.

Fuel and transportation costs are also significant deductions for rideshare drivers. Keep track of your gas receipts, tolls, parking fees, and even public transportation expenses related to your business activities. All of these costs can be deducted, ensuring you're not paying more taxes than necessary.

In today's digital age, mobile phone and internet expenses are essential for rideshare drivers. Luckily, these costs are deductible as well. Whether it's your monthly phone bill or internet fees for online navigation and communication with passengers, you can claim these expenses on your tax return.

Parking and toll fees incurred during your rideshare trips can also be deducted. Make sure to keep detailed records of these expenses to accurately reflect them on your tax return.

Vehicle depreciation and leasing expenses are another area where you can maximize deductions. If you lease a vehicle or own one that's depreciating in value, you can claim a portion of these costs based on your business usage.

Advertising and marketing expenses are deductible as well. Whether you're promoting your services through online ads, business cards, or flyers, these costs can be claimed as deductions.

Home office and workspace deductions are applicable if you use a portion of your home exclusively for your rideshare business. This includes expenses such as rent, utilities, and even depreciation of your home.

Lastly, vehicle cleaning and detailing expenses can also be claimed as deductions. From car washes to interior cleaning, these costs can be deducted to reduce your taxable income.

Understanding and utilizing these tax deductions is crucial for maximizing your earnings as an Uber, Lyft, or limousine driver. By keeping accurate records and seeking professional tax advice, you can ensure you're taking advantage of all the deductions available to you, ultimately reducing your tax liability and keeping more money in your pocket.

What is a Schedule C and why is it important for rideshare drivers

As an Uber, Lyft, or limousine driver, it's crucial to understand the importance of a Schedule C when it comes to maximizing your tax deductions. The Schedule C is a form used by the Internal Revenue Service (IRS) to report profit or loss from a business you operated or a profession you practiced as a sole proprietor. For rideshare drivers, this means reporting your earnings and expenses related to your driving business.

Why is the Schedule C important? Well, it allows you to take advantage of numerous tax deductions that can significantly reduce your taxable income and ultimately lower your tax liability. By properly documenting and categorizing your expenses, you can maximize your tax deductions and keep more money in your pocket.

One of the key areas where the Schedule C is crucial for rideshare drivers is in rideshare expenses. This includes expenses such as vehicle mileage, tolls, parking fees, and even car washes. Keeping track of these expenses and reporting them accurately on your Schedule C can lead to substantial deductions.

Another important aspect is vehicle maintenance and repairs. As a rideshare driver, your vehicle is your primary tool for making money. Any expenses related to maintaining and repairing your car, such as oil changes, tire rotations, or even major repairs, can be deducted on your Schedule C.

Insurance and licensing fees are also deductible. As a rideshare driver, you are required to have appropriate insurance coverage and licenses to operate legally. These costs can add up, but by reporting them on your Schedule C, you can reduce your tax liability.

Other areas where the Schedule C can be beneficial include fuel and transportation costs, mobile phone and internet expenses, parking and toll fees, vehicle depreciation and leasing expenses, advertising and marketing expenses, home office and workspace deductions, and even vehicle cleaning and detailing expenses.

In conclusion, the Schedule C is a critical tool for rideshare drivers to maximize their tax deductions. By properly documenting and reporting their income and expenses, drivers can significantly reduce their taxable income and lower their tax liability. Understanding the various categories where deductions can be claimed is essential for maximizing tax savings and keeping more money in your pocket.

An example of what the Schedule C Form looks like is on the next page.

Differentiating Business and Personal Expenses

As an Uber, Lyft, or limousine driver, it is crucial to understand the difference between business and personal expenses in order to maximize your tax deductions. Personal expenses are expenses you incurr that are not related to the business. A few examples include groceries, gas for personal errands, car washes for non-business trips, phone usage outside of work, gym memberships and entertainment costs while waiting on clients, (yes your Netflix, HBO and Audible subscriptions are not deductible.)

By understanding the difference between business and personal expenses and maximizing your tax deductions in various categories, you can significantly reduce your tax burden as a rideshare driver. Remember to keep accurate records and consult with a tax professional to ensure you are maximizing your deductions and staying compliant with the IRS.

Keeping Accurate Records for Tax Purposes

As an Uber, Lyft, or limousine driver, it is essential to keep accurate records for tax purposes. By doing so, you can maximize your tax deductions and potentially save a significant amount of money. In this subchapter, we will explore various areas where you can maximize tax deductions and provide tips on how to keep accurate records for each category.

1. Rideshare Expenses: Keep track of all your rideshare expenses, including tolls, parking fees, and any other costs directly related to your rideshare business. Save receipts and record the dates, amounts, and purposes of these expenses.

2. Vehicle Maintenance and Repairs: Regular maintenance and repairs on your vehicle are necessary for your rideshare business. Keep a record of all maintenance and repair expenses, such as oil changes, tire replacements, and repairs. These expenses can be deductible, so make sure to save all receipts.

3. Insurance and Licensing Fees: As a rideshare driver, you are required to have specific insurance coverage and pay licensing fees. Keep a copy of your insurance policy and record the cost of premiums and any licensing fees you incur.

4. Fuel and Transportation Costs: Fuel is a significant expense for rideshare drivers. Keep track of all your fuel expenses by saving receipts and recording the dates, amounts, and purposes of each purchase. Additionally, if you use public transportation or rideshare services for business purposes, keep a record of these expenses as well.

5. Mobile Phone and Internet Expenses: Your mobile phone and internet connection are vital tools for your rideshare business. Keep records of your phone and internet bills, as these expenses can be deductible. If you use your phone for personal and business purposes, make sure to allocate the business portion of the expenses.

6. Parking and Toll Fees: Parking fees and tolls can quickly add up for rideshare drivers. Save receipts and record the dates, amounts, and purposes of these expenses. These costs are generally deductible, so keeping accurate records is essential.

7. Vehicle Depreciation and Leasing Expenses: If you own or lease your vehicle for your rideshare business, you can deduct depreciation or lease payments. Keep records of your vehicle purchase or lease agreement, along with any associated expenses.

8. Advertising and Marketing Expenses: As a rideshare driver, you may incur expenses for advertising and marketing your services. Keep a record of these expenses, such as business cards, flyers, or online advertising costs.

9. Home Office and Workspace Deductions: If you use a portion of your home exclusively for your rideshare business, you may qualify for a home office deduction. Keep records of your home office expenses, such as rent, utilities, and home office supplies.

10. Vehicle Cleaning and Detailing Expenses: Maintaining a clean vehicle is essential for your rideshare business. Keep receipts and records of any expenses related to vehicle cleaning and detailing, as they can be deductible.

By keeping accurate records for tax purposes, you can maximize your tax deductions and potentially reduce your tax liability as an Uber, Lyft, or limousine driver. Remember to save all receipts, record expenses regularly, and consult a tax professional to ensure you take advantage of all available deductions.

Chapter 2: Maximizing Tax Deductions - Standard Mileage Method

What is the standard mileage method from the IRS and what expenses does it cover

What is the standard mileage method from the IRS and what expenses does it cover?

As a rideshare driver, it is crucial to understand the standard mileage method from the IRS and the expenses it covers. By utilizing this method effectively, you can maximize your tax deductions and ultimately reduce your overall tax liability.

The standard mileage method is a simplified way to calculate your deductible vehicle expenses based on the number of miles you drive for business purposes. Instead of tracking and deducting individual expenses, such as gas, insurance, and maintenance, you can simply multiply the total business miles driven by the standard mileage rate set by the IRS.

For the tax year 2023, the standard mileage rate is 65.5 cents per mile for business miles driven (rising to 67 cents per mile for 2024.) This rate covers various expenses related to your vehicle, including fuel and transportation costs, vehicle maintenance and repairs, insurance and licensing fees, vehicle depreciation and leasing expenses, and even parking and toll fees. For example if you drove 10,000 total business miles in 2023 you can deduct (10,000* $0.655) $6550.

However, it is important to note that the standard mileage method does not cover all expenses incurred while driving for Uber or any other rideshare service. For instance, it does not include mobile phone and internet expenses, advertising and marketing expenses, or home office and workspace deductions.

To maximize your tax deductions, it is essential to keep detailed records of all your business-related expenses. This includes maintaining a mileage log that documents the date, purpose, and number of miles driven for each business trip. Additionally, you should retain receipts and invoices for any expenses not covered by the standard mileage rate.

By understanding the standard mileage method and leveraging it effectively, you can ensure that you are accurately deducting your vehicle-related expenses while minimizing the risk of an IRS audit. Consulting with a tax professional who specializes in working with rideshare drivers can provide further guidance and ensure that you are taking advantage of all available deductions.

In conclusion, the standard mileage method offered by the IRS is a simplified approach to deducting vehicle expenses for Uber, Lyft, and limousine drivers. It covers various costs, such as fuel, maintenance, insurance, and licensing fees, based on the number of business miles driven. However, it does not include certain expenses like mobile phone and internet costs, advertising and marketing expenses, or home office deductions. Because of its inherent limitations it might not be the most advantageous for you. Consult a tax expert for clarity.

How to keep track of miles driven

As an rideshare driver, keeping track of the miles you drive is crucial for maximizing your tax deductions. The IRS allows you to deduct a certain amount per mile driven for business purposes, so it's important to accurately track your mileage to ensure you receive the maximum deductions possible. In this subchapter, we will explore different methods and tools that can help you keep track of your miles driven.

One of the easiest ways to track your mileage is by using a mileage tracking app. There are several apps available specifically designed for rideshare drivers, such as MileIQ, TripLog, and Everlance. These apps use GPS technology to automatically track your trips, making it effortless for you to log your miles. They also provide detailed reports that you can easily export for tax purposes.

Alternatively, you can use a mileage logbook to manually record your miles. Keep this logbook in your vehicle and make it a habit to note down the date, starting and ending odometer readings, and the purpose of each trip. This method requires more effort and discipline but can be just as effective.

Another method to consider is using a GPS mileage tracker. These devices can be easily installed in your vehicle and automatically record your miles as you drive. They often come with features such as real-time tracking, which can be useful for planning your routes and maximizing your efficiency.

It's important to note that the IRS requires you to keep accurate records of your mileage. This means that you should record both your business and personal miles separately. For example, if you use your vehicle for personal errands, you should only deduct the miles driven for business purposes.

In addition to keeping track of your miles, it's also important to keep receipts and documentation for any related expenses, such as fuel, maintenance, and repairs. This will help you maximize your deductions and provide proof to the IRS if needed.

By diligently tracking your miles driven and maintaining proper documentation, you can maximize your tax deductions as an Uber, Lyft, or limousine driver. Remember to consult with a tax professional or accountant who specializes in rideshare taxes to ensure you are taking advantage of all available deductions and staying compliant with IRS regulations.

Which miles are eligible to be included in the calculation

It is essential to understand which miles are eligible to be included in the calculation of your tax deductions. By accurately tracking and categorizing your miles, you can maximize your tax deductions and minimize your tax liability. In this subchapter, we will explore the different types of miles that can be included in your calculation.

1. Maximize tax deductions for Uber drivers in rideshare expenses:
- All miles driven while actively transporting passengers for Uber, Lyft, or other rideshare services are eligible for deduction.
- This includes miles driven to pick up passengers, miles driven with passengers in the car, and miles driven to drop off passengers.

2. Maximize tax deductions for Uber drivers in vehicle maintenance and repairs:
- Any miles driven for the purpose of vehicle maintenance and repairs are eligible for deduction.
- This includes miles driven to the mechanic, auto parts store, or car wash.

3. Maximize tax deductions for Uber drivers in insurance and licensing fees:
- Miles driven for the purpose of obtaining or renewing insurance and licensing are eligible for deduction.
- This includes miles driven to the Department of Motor Vehicles (DMV), insurance agency, or any other relevant government office.

4. Maximize tax deductions for Uber drivers in fuel and transportation costs:
- All miles driven for the purpose of purchasing fuel or paying for transportation costs are eligible for deduction.
- This includes miles driven to the gas station, public transportation stations, or car rental agencies.

5. Maximize tax deductions for Uber drivers in mobile phone and internet expenses:
- Miles driven for the purpose of purchasing or maintaining your mobile phone and internet services are eligible for deduction.
- This includes miles driven to the phone or internet service provider's store.

6. Maximize tax deductions for Uber drivers in parking and toll fees:
- All miles driven for the purpose of paying for parking or toll fees are eligible for deduction.
- This includes miles driven to parking lots, garages, or toll booths.

7. Maximize tax deductions for Uber drivers in vehicle depreciation and leasing expenses:
- Miles driven for the purpose of vehicle depreciation or leasing expenses are eligible for deduction.
- This includes miles driven to leasing agencies or any other relevant location for vehicle-related expenses.

8. Maximize tax deductions for Uber drivers in advertising and marketing expenses:
- Miles driven for the purpose of advertising and marketing your services as an Uber driver are eligible for deduction.
- This includes miles driven to distribute flyers, attend networking events, or place advertisements.

9. Maximize tax deductions for Uber drivers in home office and workspace deductions:
- Miles driven for the purpose of maintaining your home office or workspace are eligible for deduction.
- This includes miles driven to purchase office supplies or attend meetings related to your business.

10. Maximize tax deductions for Uber drivers in vehicle cleaning and detailing expenses:

- Miles driven for the purpose of cleaning and detailing your vehicle are eligible for deduction.
- This includes miles driven to car washes, auto detailing shops, or purchasing cleaning supplies.

Remember, accurate record-keeping is crucial when it comes to claiming these deductions. Utilize mileage tracking apps or keep a detailed logbook to ensure you have the necessary documentation to support your deductions.

By understanding which miles are eligible to be included in the calculation, you can take full advantage of the tax deductions available to you as an Uber, Lyft, or limousine driver. Properly tracking and categorizing your miles will help you maximize your deductions and ultimately reduce your tax liability.

Chapter 3: Maximizing Tax Deductions - Actual Expense Method

What is the Actual Expense Method and what expenses does it cover

What is the Actual Expense Method and what expenses does it cover?

As an Uber, Lyft, or limousine driver, it is crucial to understand the various tax deductions available to you in order to maximize your earnings. One of the most important methods for calculating your deductible expenses is the Actual Expense Method. In this subchapter, we will delve into what the Actual Expense Method entails and the different expenses it covers.

The Actual Expense Method allows you to deduct the actual costs associated with using your vehicle for business purposes. This means that you can deduct a wide range of expenses related to your rideshare business, which can significantly reduce your taxable income.

Under this method, you can deduct expenses such as vehicle maintenance and repairs. This includes the costs of regular maintenance, oil changes, tire rotations, and any repairs necessary to keep your vehicle in good working condition. Additionally, you can deduct insurance premiums and licensing fees required for your rideshare business.

Fuel and transportation costs are also deductible expenses. You can deduct the cost of gasoline, diesel, or any other fuel used for your rideshare trips. Additionally, expenses related to public transportation, such as bus or train fares, can also be deducted.

As an Uber driver, your mobile phone and internet expenses are essential for staying connected and receiving ride requests. These expenses can be deducted under the Actual Expense Method. Similarly, parking fees and tolls incurred during your rideshare trips can also be deducted.

Vehicle depreciation and leasing expenses are significant deductions for rideshare drivers. You can deduct a portion of the cost of purchasing or leasing your vehicle, as well as any interest payments on a car loan.

Advertising and marketing expenses are another important deduction. If you spend money on promoting your rideshare business, such as creating business cards or online advertisements, these expenses can be deducted.

Home office and workspace deductions are available to drivers who use a designated area of their home for administrative tasks related to their rideshare business. This can include a portion of your rent or mortgage, utilities, and other home office expenses.

Lastly, vehicle cleaning and detailing expenses can also be deducted. As a rideshare driver, it is essential to maintain a clean and presentable vehicle for your passengers. The costs associated with cleaning supplies, car washes, and detailing services can be deducted.

In conclusion, the Actual Expense Method allows Uber, Lyft, and limousine drivers to deduct a wide range of expenses related to their rideshare business. By understanding and utilizing these deductions, you can maximize your tax deductions and ultimately increase your take-home earnings.

What expenses are not eligible for the Actual Expense Method

As an Uber, Lyft, or limousine driver, you have the opportunity to maximize your tax deductions and save money on your annual tax bill. One of the methods you can use is the Actual Expense Method, which allows you to deduct the actual costs associated with your business. However, it's important to know that not all expenses are eligible for this method. In this subchapter, we will explore what expenses are not eligible for the Actual Expense Method, so you can make informed decisions when filing your taxes.

1. Personal Expenses: Expenses that are purely personal and not related to your business as a rideshare driver are not eligible for deduction. This includes personal meals, entertainment, vacations, and other non-business-related expenses.

2. Fines and Penalties: Any fines or penalties you incur while driving, such as parking tickets or traffic violations, cannot be deducted as a business expense.

3. Commuting Expenses: The expenses you incur while commuting to and from your home to pick up passengers are not eligible for deduction. This includes fuel costs, toll fees, and parking fees during your regular commute.

4. Non-business Use of Vehicle: If you use your vehicle for personal purposes, such as running errands or going on personal trips, you cannot deduct the expenses associated with those trips. Only the expenses directly related to your business activities are eligible for deduction.

5. Personal Vehicle Maintenance and Repairs: While you can deduct the expenses for maintaining and repairing your vehicle for business purposes, any maintenance or repairs that are solely for personal use are not eligible for deduction.

6. Personal Insurance and Licensing Fees: If you have personal insurance coverage or licensing fees that are not directly related to your business as a rideshare driver, they cannot be deducted as business expenses.

7. Non-business Mobile Phone and Internet Expenses: If you use your mobile phone or internet for personal purposes, you cannot deduct the full cost. Only

the portion of these expenses that are directly related to your business can be deducted.

It is essential to keep accurate records of your expenses and consult with a tax professional to ensure you are claiming the appropriate deductions and complying with the tax regulations. Understanding what expenses are not eligible for the Actual Expense Method will help you maximize your tax deductions and keep more money in your pocket.

Chapter 4: Other Expenses deductible under Actual Expense Method

Vehicle Maintenance and Repair Deductions

As an Uber, Lyft, or limousine driver, maximizing your tax deductions is essential to keeping more money in your pocket. One significant area where you can save money is in vehicle maintenance and repair expenses. By understanding the tax deductions available to you in this category, you can reduce your taxable income and increase your overall tax savings.

When it comes to vehicle maintenance and repairs, there are several expenses that you can potentially deduct. These include costs for regular tune-ups, oil changes, tire rotations, and other routine maintenance to keep your vehicle in top shape. Additionally, any repairs necessary to fix mechanical issues or accidents can also be deducted.

To ensure that you are maximizing your deductions, it's important to keep detailed records of all your vehicle expenses. This includes receipts for parts, labor, and any other related costs. By organizing and documenting these expenses, you will have the necessary evidence to support your deductions during tax season.

It's also worth noting that you can deduct expenses for insurance and licensing fees associated with your vehicle. This includes both personal and commercial insurance policies, as well as any fees required to obtain or renew your driver's license or commercial driving license.

Furthermore, fuel and transportation costs are deductible as well. Keep track of all your fuel purchases and any expenses related to public transportation or rideshare services used for business purposes. These costs can quickly add up, so it's essential to keep accurate records.

In today's digital age, mobile phone and internet expenses are unavoidable for Uber, Lyft, and limousine drivers. The good news is that these costs can also be deducted. Whether you're using your smartphone for navigation or your internet connection to communicate with passengers, be sure to include these expenses when calculating your deductions.

Parking and toll fees are another area where you can save money. Keep track of any parking fees incurred while waiting for passengers or tolls paid during business-related trips. These expenses can add up over time and can make a significant impact on your tax savings.

Lastly, vehicle depreciation and leasing expenses, advertising and marketing expenses, home office and workspace deductions, and vehicle cleaning and detailing expenses are all potential deductions that you should be aware of. The more you educate yourself about the available deductions, the more money you can save.

In conclusion, vehicle maintenance and repair deductions are a crucial aspect of maximizing your tax savings as an Uber, Lyft, or limousine driver. By keeping accurate records and understanding the deductions available to you, you can significantly reduce your taxable income and increase your overall tax deductions. Take the time to educate yourself on the specific requirements and guidelines set forth by the IRS, and consult with a qualified tax professional to ensure you are taking full advantage of all the deductions available to you.

Fuel and Transportation Costs Deductions

As an Uber, Lyft, or limousine driver, one of your biggest expenses is fuel and transportation costs. However, the good news is that you may be eligible to claim tax deductions for these expenses, helping you maximize your savings and minimize your tax liability. In this subchapter, we will explore the various deductions available to you in this category.

First and foremost, it is important to keep detailed records of all your fuel expenses. This includes receipts for gasoline, diesel, or any other fuel you use for your vehicle while working as a rideshare driver. These expenses can be deducted in full, so make sure to retain all relevant receipts and log your mileage accurately.

In addition to fuel costs, you can also deduct other transportation-related expenses. This includes toll fees, parking fees, and even public transportation fares incurred while driving for Uber, Lyft, or as a limousine driver. These expenses are fully deductible as long as they are directly related to your rideshare business.

Furthermore, if you use your personal vehicle for work purposes, you may be eligible for additional deductions. This includes expenses for vehicle maintenance and repairs, such as oil changes, tire rotations, and brake replacements. Additionally, insurance premiums and licensing fees can also be deducted. Just make sure to keep thorough records and only claim the portion of these expenses that is directly related to your rideshare business.

Lastly, if you use a mobile phone or internet connection for your rideshare business, you can deduct a portion of these expenses as well. This is particularly relevant for Uber, Lyft, and limousine drivers who rely heavily on these tools for communication and navigation. Similarly, if you have a dedicated home office or workspace for managing your rideshare business, you may be able to claim deductions for expenses related to it.

In conclusion, fuel and transportation costs can be significant for Uber, Lyft, and limousine drivers. However, by understanding and utilizing the available tax deductions in this category, you can effectively lower your taxable income and maximize your savings. Remember to keep detailed records, consult with a tax professional, and take advantage of every eligible deduction to optimize your tax situation as a rideshare driver.

Insurance and Licensing Fees Deductions

As an Uber, Lyft, or limousine driver, one of the most important aspects of your business is ensuring that you have adequate insurance coverage and the necessary licenses to operate legally. However, these expenses can add up quickly and have a significant impact on your bottom line. The good news is that you may be eligible to deduct these costs on your taxes, allowing you to maximize your savings and keep more money in your pocket.

When it comes to insurance, you can deduct the premiums you pay for liability coverage, comprehensive coverage, and collision coverage. These expenses are considered necessary for the operation of your business and are therefore deductible. Additionally, if you have any additional insurance policies, such as umbrella policies or rideshare endorsements, you may be able to deduct the premiums for these as well.

In addition to insurance, you can also deduct any licensing fees you incur as part of your business. This includes fees for obtaining and renewing your driver's license, as well as any fees associated with obtaining or renewing a commercial driver's license. These fees are directly related to your ability to operate as a rideshare driver, so they are considered necessary and deductible expenses.

It's important to note that in order to claim these deductions, you must keep detailed records of your insurance premiums and licensing fees. This includes keeping copies of your insurance policies, receipts for premium payments, and any correspondence related to your licensing fees. These records will be crucial in the event of an audit, so it's important to keep them organized and easily accessible.

By taking advantage of the insurance and licensing fees deductions, you can significantly reduce your tax liability and increase your overall profitability as an Uber, Lyft, or limousine driver. However, it's always a good idea to consult with a qualified tax professional or accountant to ensure that you are maximizing your deductions and taking advantage of any other tax-saving strategies that may be available to you. With their expertise, you can navigate the complex world of tax deductions and keep more of your hard-earned money in your pocket.

Tracking and Documenting Mobile Phone and Internet Expenses

As an Uber, Lyft, or limousine driver, you rely heavily on your mobile phone and internet connection to run your business effectively. Whether it's communicating with passengers, navigating through traffic, or accessing the Uber app, your mobile phone and internet expenses are integral to your daily operations. The good news is that these expenses can be tax-deductible, allowing you to maximize your deductions and lower your tax liability.

To ensure you receive the maximum tax deductions for your mobile phone and internet expenses, it's crucial to track and document these costs accurately. Here are some tips to help you navigate this process:

1. Separate Business and Personal Use: To claim a deduction for your mobile phone and internet expenses, you must establish the percentage of business use. Keep a record of the time spent on business-related activities versus personal use. This can be easily done by using apps or software that track your phone and internet usage.

2. Keep Detailed Records: Maintain records of all your mobile phone and internet bills, including receipts and invoices. These documents should clearly show the amount, date, and purpose of each expense. You can also consider creating a dedicated folder or digital file to store all these records for easy access during tax season.

3. Choose the Right Plan: Opt for a mobile phone and internet plan that suits your business needs. If you use your phone primarily for business purposes, consider choosing a plan that offers unlimited data or a higher data limit. This way, you can ensure that your expenses accurately reflect your business usage.

4. Consider a Separate Business Line: If you use your personal phone for both business and personal purposes, it may be beneficial to set up a separate business line. This will make it easier to differentiate and track your business-related calls and internet usage.

5. Consult with a Tax Professional: Tax laws and regulations can be complex, especially when it comes to deductions for mobile phone and internet expenses. To ensure you are maximizing your deductions and complying with all requirements, it's advisable to consult with a tax professional who specializes in rideshare drivers.

By diligently tracking and documenting your mobile phone and internet expenses, you can maximize your tax deductions and potentially save a significant amount of money. Remember, every dollar you save on taxes is a dollar that stays in your pocket, so make sure to take advantage of all the deductions available to you as an Uber, Lyft, or limousine driver.

Identifying Deductible Toll Fees and Parking Expenses

As an Uber, Lyft, or limousine driver, you are well aware of the myriad of expenses that come with operating your own business. From vehicle maintenance to fuel costs, it can be overwhelming to keep track of everything. However, one area that is often overlooked but can provide significant tax deductions is toll fees and parking expenses.

Toll fees are a common occurrence for rideshare drivers, especially when navigating busy highways or crossing bridges. The good news is that these costs can be deducted from your taxable income, reducing your overall tax liability. To ensure you claim these deductions accurately, it's important to keep a record of each toll fee paid. This includes receipts, electronic statements, or any other documentation that verifies the expense.

Similarly, parking expenses incurred while working as a rideshare driver can also be deducted. Whether it's parking at airports, hotels, or other designated areas, these costs can add up over time. Just like toll fees, it is crucial to keep detailed records of each parking expense. This can be done by saving receipts, taking pictures of parking meters, or using mobile apps that track your parking expenses.

To maximize your tax deductions for toll fees and parking expenses, it is recommended to use a mileage tracking app or software. These tools not only help you keep track of your business-related mileage but can also record toll fees and parking expenses automatically, saving you time and effort when tax season comes around.

Additionally, it is crucial to consult with a tax professional who specializes in rideshare driver deductions. They can provide expert advice on how to accurately claim toll fees and parking expenses, ensuring you receive the maximum deductions allowed by law.

Remember, every dollar saved in tax deductions is a dollar that stays in your pocket. By identifying and claiming deductible toll fees and parking expenses, you can effectively reduce your overall tax liability and maximize your earnings as an Uber, Lyft, or limousine driver.

In conclusion, toll fees and parking expenses are often overlooked but can provide significant tax deductions for rideshare drivers. By keeping detailed records, utilizing mileage tracking apps, and seeking professional advice, you can ensure you are claiming these deductions accurately and maximizing your tax savings.

Advertising and Marketing Expenses

As an Uber, Lyft, or limousine driver, one of the key aspects of running a successful business is effectively advertising and marketing your services. Fortunately, the expenses associated with these activities can be tax deductible, allowing you to maximize your tax deductions and potentially save money. In this subchapter, we will explore the various advertising and marketing expenses that you can deduct as an Uber driver.

When it comes to advertising, there are several strategies you can employ to attract more passengers and increase your earnings. You may choose to invest in online advertising platforms, such as Google Ads or social media advertising, to promote your services to a wider audience. These advertising expenses can be deducted as long as they are directly related to your business.

Additionally, traditional marketing methods like printing flyers, business cards, or brochures can also be deducted. If you attend trade shows or events to promote your services, the expenses incurred, such as booth rentals or promotional materials, can also be deducted.

It's important to note that any expenses related to creating and maintaining your professional website can also be deducted. This includes the cost of domain registration, web hosting fees, and website design or development expenses.

Furthermore, expenses associated with branding and logo design can be deducted as well. This includes hiring graphic designers or marketing agencies to create your logo, business name, or any other branding materials.

To ensure that you can claim these deductions, it's essential to keep detailed records of all your advertising and marketing expenses. This includes saving receipts, invoices, and any other relevant documentation. By doing so, you can provide evidence of these expenses in case of an audit.

Remember, maximizing your tax deductions is crucial for Uber drivers to minimize their tax liability and keep more money in their pockets. By understanding and utilizing the deductions available for advertising and marketing expenses, you can effectively promote your services while also saving money on your taxes.

In the following chapters, we will delve into other areas where you can maximize your tax deductions as an Uber driver, including rideshare expenses, vehicle maintenance and repairs, insurance and licensing fees, fuel and transportation costs, mobile phone and internet expenses, parking and toll fees, vehicle depreciation and leasing expenses, home office and workspace deductions, and vehicle cleaning and detailing expenses. Stay tuned for more tips and strategies to help you maximize your tax deductions and boost your profits as an Uber driver.

Deductible Vehicle Cleaning Expenses

As a rideshare driver, it's important to take advantage of every possible tax deduction available to you. One often overlooked area where you may be able to maximize your deductions is in vehicle cleaning expenses. In this subchapter, we will explore how you can deduct these expenses and ensure that you are getting the most out of your tax return.

Vehicle cleaning and detailing expenses are considered ordinary and necessary expenses for your business as a rideshare driver. This means that you can deduct the costs associated with keeping your vehicle clean and presentable for your passengers. These expenses include car washes, interior cleaning, vacuuming, and even professional detailing services.

To qualify for this deduction, you must be able to prove that these expenses are directly related to your business as a rideshare driver. This can be done by keeping detailed records of your cleaning expenses, including receipts, invoices, and a log of when and why you had your vehicle cleaned. It's also a good idea to take before and after photos of your vehicle to show the condition it was in before and after cleaning.

It's important to note that personal use of your vehicle may limit the amount you can deduct for cleaning expenses. If you use your vehicle for personal purposes as well, you will need to allocate the expenses between business and personal use. This can be done by determining the percentage of time your vehicle is used for business purposes and applying that percentage to the total cleaning expenses.

In addition to regular cleaning expenses, you may also be able to deduct the cost of any cleaning supplies or equipment you purchase specifically for your rideshare business. This can include items such as car cleaning products, vacuum cleaners, and even air fresheners. Again, it's important to keep detailed records and receipts for these purchases.

By taking advantage of the deduction for vehicle cleaning expenses, you can potentially save a significant amount of money on your taxes. However, it's important to consult with a tax professional or use tax software specifically designed for rideshare drivers to ensure that you are maximizing your deductions and staying compliant with tax laws.

In conclusion, as an Uber, Lyft, or limousine driver, you can deduct vehicle cleaning expenses as ordinary and necessary expenses for your business. By keeping detailed records and receipts, allocating expenses between business and personal use, and taking advantage of deductions for cleaning supplies and equipment, you can maximize your tax deductions and potentially save a significant amount of money. Don't overlook this often forgotten deduction and make sure to consult with a tax professional or use tax software to ensure you are getting the most out of your tax return.

Business-related meals and snacks for driver and passengers

Business-related meals and snacks for drivers and passengers are often overlooked when it comes to tax deductions for Uber, Lyft, and limousine drivers. However, understanding the rules and maximizing these deductions can help you save significant amounts of money. In this subchapter, we will explore how you can maximize tax deductions for these expenses and ensure that you are getting the most out of your ridesharing business.

As an Uber driver, meals and snacks are an inevitable part of your workday. Whether it's grabbing a quick bite to eat between rides or providing refreshments for your passengers, these expenses can add up over time. The good news is that you can deduct 50% of your business-related meal and snack expenses, as long as they are directly related to your ridesharing activities.

To qualify for this deduction, you must be able to prove that the meals and snacks were necessary for your business. This can be done by keeping detailed records of your expenses, including receipts, dates, and the business purpose of each meal or snack. It is also important to note that extravagant or lavish expenses may not be fully deductible, so it's best to stick to reasonable and necessary costs.

When it comes to providing meals and snacks for your passengers, you can also deduct these expenses. Whether you offer bottled water, snacks, or even a fully stocked mini-fridge, these costs can be claimed as a business expense. Again, it is crucial to keep records of the expenses and the business purpose of providing these amenities to your passengers.

It's important to remember that personal meals and snacks are not deductible. Only expenses directly related to your ridesharing business can be claimed. Additionally, it's a good idea to consult with a tax professional or refer to the IRS guidelines to ensure that you are complying with all the necessary requirements.

By taking advantage of the tax deductions available for business-related meals and snacks, you can significantly reduce your taxable income and ultimately save money. As a rideshare driver, every dollar counts, and maximizing your deductions is an essential part of running a profitable business. So, don't overlook these expenses and make sure to keep accurate records to take full advantage of this deduction.

Health Insurance for the driver

As an Uber, Lyft, or limousine driver, it is crucial to ensure that you have adequate health insurance coverage. This subchapter will provide you with essential information on how to maximize tax deductions for health insurance expenses, ensuring that you protect yourself and your financial well-being.

Health insurance is a necessary expense for any individual, especially for those in the transportation industry. As an independent contractor, you are responsible for your own health insurance coverage, unlike traditional employees who may receive benefits through their employer. However, the good news is that you can deduct health insurance premiums as a business expense, lowering your overall tax liability.

To maximize tax deductions for health insurance expenses, it is important to understand the eligibility criteria set by the Internal Revenue Service (IRS). Generally, you can deduct health insurance premiums if you meet the following conditions:

1. You are not eligible to participate in a subsidized health insurance plan offered by your spouse's employer.

2. You are not eligible to participate in any other employer-sponsored health insurance plan.

3. You are not eligible for coverage through a government program like Medicare or Medicaid.

If you meet these criteria, you can deduct your health insurance premiums as an adjustment to income on your tax return, reducing your taxable income.

This deduction is available whether you purchase health insurance through the marketplace or directly from an insurance company.

It is important to keep detailed records of your health insurance expenses, including receipts and invoices. These records will serve as evidence in case of an audit by the IRS. Additionally, it is advisable to consult with a tax professional or accountant who specializes in working with rideshare drivers to ensure that you are taking full advantage of all available deductions.

In conclusion, health insurance is a critical aspect of your financial security as a rideshare driver. By understanding and maximizing tax deductions for health insurance expenses, you can protect yourself and your business while reducing your overall tax liability. Remember to keep accurate records and seek professional guidance to ensure compliance with IRS regulations.

Rideshare Commissions

As an Uber, Lyft, or limousine driver, one of the key aspects of your business is understanding and maximizing your tax deductions. One area that often gets overlooked is rideshare commissions. In this subchapter, we will explore how you can maximize your deductions in this area and keep more money in your pocket.

When driving for a rideshare platform, such as Uber or Lyft, you are required to pay a commission or service fee on each trip. These fees can add up quickly and eat into your earnings. However, the good news is that you can deduct these commissions as a business expense, reducing your taxable income.

To maximize your deductions in this area, it is important to keep detailed records of the commissions you pay. Make sure to save all your receipts and statements from the rideshare platform, as these will serve as proof of your expenses. You can also use expense tracking software or apps to help you stay organized and ensure you don't miss any deductions.

In addition to the commissions you pay, don't forget to include any other related fees or charges. This could include booking fees, safety fees, or any other expenses directly related to your rideshare business. All these expenses can add up and significantly reduce your taxable income.

It is also worth noting that if you use a third-party service to manage your rideshare business, such as a dispatch or booking service, you can also deduct the fees you pay to them. These fees are considered a necessary expense for running your business and can be included in your deductions.

Remember, maximizing your tax deductions is crucial for Uber, Lyft, and limousine drivers to minimize their tax liability and keep more of their hard-earned money. By properly documenting and deducting your rideshare commissions and related expenses, you can ensure that you are taking full advantage of all available deductions.

In conclusion, rideshare commissions are a significant expense for Uber, Lyft, and limousine drivers. By keeping meticulous records and including all related fees and charges, you can maximize your deductions and reduce your taxable income. Don't overlook this important aspect of your business, as it can make a significant difference in your overall tax liability.

Chapter 5: Maximizing Tax Deductions in Vehicle Depreciation and Leasing Expenses

Depreciation Deductions for Uber Drivers

As an Uber, Lyft, or limousine driver, you are considered a self-employed individual. This means that you have the opportunity to take advantage of several tax deductions that can significantly reduce your overall tax liability. One of the most valuable deductions available to you is depreciation.

Depreciation allows you to recover the cost of your vehicle over time, recognizing that its value decreases as it is used. This deduction can be a significant benefit for rideshare drivers like yourself, as your car is an essential tool for your business.

To maximize your depreciation deductions, there are a few key factors to consider. First, you need to determine the cost basis of your vehicle. This includes the purchase price, sales tax, and any other fees associated with acquiring the vehicle.

Next, you need to determine the useful life of your vehicle. The IRS provides guidelines for different types of vehicles, and you can use these guidelines to determine how many years you can depreciate your vehicle. For most passenger vehicles used for business purposes, the useful life is five years.

Once you have determined the cost basis and useful life, you can calculate your annual depreciation deduction. This is typically done using a method called Modified Accelerated Cost Recovery System (MACRS).

It's important to note that there are limits to the amount of depreciation you can deduct each year. The IRS sets a maximum depreciation deduction based on the cost basis and the useful life of your vehicle. However, in many cases, this limit will not be reached, allowing you to deduct the full amount of your depreciation.

In addition to the standard depreciation deduction, there are also special rules that apply to luxury vehicles. If your vehicle exceeds a certain value, you may be subject to additional limitations on your depreciation deductions.

To ensure you are maximizing your depreciation deductions, it is highly recommended that you consult with a tax professional who specializes in rideshare drivers. They can help you navigate the complex tax laws and ensure you are taking full advantage of all available deductions.

Overall, depreciation deductions can be a significant benefit for Uber, Lyft, and limousine drivers. By properly calculating and claiming your depreciation deductions, you can reduce your tax liability and maximize your overall tax savings.

Form 4562 explained

As an Uber, Lyft, or limousine driver, maximizing your tax deductions is crucial to maximizing your income. One of the most important forms you need to understand is Form 4562. In this subchapter, we will explain what Form 4562 is and how it can help you maximize your tax deductions.

Form 4562, also known as the Depreciation and Amortization form, is used to report depreciation and amortization expenses for business assets. As a rideshare driver, your vehicle is one of your most important assets, and understanding how to deduct its expenses is essential.

Maximizing tax deductions for Uber drivers in rideshare expenses starts with properly calculating the depreciation of your vehicle. Form 4562 allows you to deduct a portion of the cost of your vehicle each year based on its useful life. This deduction can significantly reduce your taxable income and lower your overall tax liability.

In addition to vehicle depreciation, Form 4562 also allows you to deduct other vehicle-related expenses. These include vehicle maintenance and repairs, insurance and licensing fees, fuel and transportation costs, parking and toll fees, and even vehicle cleaning and detailing expenses. By carefully tracking and documenting these expenses, you can maximize your deductions and keep more money in your pocket.

But Form 4562 doesn't stop at vehicle-related deductions. It also allows you to deduct other business expenses, such as mobile phone and internet expenses, advertising and marketing expenses, and even home office and workspace deductions. These deductions can further reduce your tax liability and help you maximize your income as a rideshare driver.

Understanding and properly completing Form 4562 can be complex, especially if you're unfamiliar with tax laws and regulations. That's why it's important to consult with a tax professional or use tax software specifically designed for rideshare drivers. These resources can guide you through the process and help ensure you're taking advantage of all available deductions.

In conclusion, Form 4562 is a powerful tool for maximizing tax deductions for Uber, Lyft, and limousine drivers. By properly calculating and documenting your vehicle-related expenses and other business expenses, you can significantly lower your tax liability and increase your overall income. Take the time to understand and utilize Form 4562 to its full potential and watch your tax savings grow.

A visual presentation of Form 4562 is on the next 2 pages

Form **4562**	**Depreciation and Amortization**	OMB No. 1545-0172
	(Including Information on Listed Property)	**2022**
Department of the Treasury Internal Revenue Service	Attach to your tax return. Go to *www.irs.gov/Form4562* for instructions and the latest information.	Attachment Sequence No. **179**
Name(s) shown on return	Business or activity to which this form relates	Identifying number

Part I   Election To Expense Certain Property Under Section 179

Note: If you have any listed property, complete Part V before you complete Part I.

1	Maximum amount (see instructions)	1
2	Total cost of section 179 property placed in service (see instructions)	2
3	Threshold cost of section 179 property before reduction in limitation (see instructions)	3
4	Reduction in limitation. Subtract line 3 from line 2. If zero or less, enter -0-	4
5	Dollar limitation for tax year. Subtract line 4 from line 1. If zero or less, enter -0-. If married filing separately, see instructions	5

6	(a) Description of property	(b) Cost (business use only)	(c) Elected cost	

7	Listed property. Enter the amount from line 29	7	
8	Total elected cost of section 179 property. Add amounts in column (c), lines 6 and 7	8
9	Tentative deduction. Enter the **smaller** of line 5 or line 8	9
10	Carryover of disallowed deduction from line 13 of your 2021 Form 4562	10
11	Business income limitation. Enter the smaller of business income (not less than zero) or line 5. See instructions	11
12	Section 179 expense deduction. Add lines 9 and 10, but don't enter more than line 11	12
13	Carryover of disallowed deduction to 2023. Add lines 9 and 10, less line 12 . .	13	

Note: Don't use Part II or Part III below for listed property. Instead, use Part V.

Part II   Special Depreciation Allowance and Other Depreciation (Don't include listed property. See instructions.)

14	Special depreciation allowance for qualified property (other than listed property) placed in service during the tax year. See instructions	14
15	Property subject to section 168(f)(1) election	15
16	Other depreciation (including ACRS)	16

Part III   MACRS Depreciation (Don't include listed property. See instructions.)

Section A

17	MACRS deductions for assets placed in service in tax years beginning before 2022	17
18	If you are electing to group any assets placed in service during the tax year into one or more general asset accounts, check here . . . . ☐	

Section B—Assets Placed in Service During 2022 Tax Year Using the General Depreciation System

(a) Classification of property	(b) Month and year placed in service	(c) Basis for depreciation (business/investment use only—see instructions)	(d) Recovery period	(e) Convention	(f) Method	(g) Depreciation deduction
19a 3-year property						
b 5-year property						
c 7-year property						
d 10-year property						
e 15-year property						
f 20-year property						
g 25-year property			25 yrs.		S/L	
h Residential rental property			27.5 yrs.	MM	S/L	
			27.5 yrs.	MM	S/L	
i Nonresidential real property			39 yrs.	MM	S/L	
				MM	S/L	

Section C—Assets Placed in Service During 2022 Tax Year Using the Alternative Depreciation System

20a Class life					S/L	
b 12-year			12 yrs.		S/L	
c 30-year			30 yrs.	MM	S/L	
d 40-year			40 yrs.	MM	S/L	

Part IV   Summary (See instructions.)

21	Listed property. Enter amount from line 28	21
22	**Total.** Add amounts from line 12, lines 14 through 17, lines 19 and 20 in column (g), and line 21. Enter here and on the appropriate lines of your return. Partnerships and S corporations—see instructions .	22
23	For assets shown above and placed in service during the current year, enter the portion of the basis attributable to section 263A costs	23	

For Paperwork Reduction Act Notice, see separate instructions.   Cat. No. 12906N   Form **4562** (2022)

Part V   **Listed Property** (Include automobiles, certain other vehicles, certain aircraft, and property used for entertainment, recreation, or amusement.)

Note: For any vehicle for which you are using the standard mileage rate or deducting lease expense, complete **only** 24a, 24b, columns (a) through (c) of Section A, all of Section B, and Section C if applicable.

Section A—Depreciation and Other Information (Caution: See the instructions for limits for passenger automobiles.)

24a Do you have evidence to support the business/investment use claimed? ☐ Yes ☐ No   24b If "Yes," is the evidence written? ☐ Yes ☐ No

(a) Type of property (list vehicles first)	(b) Date placed in service	(c) Business/ investment use percentage	(d) Cost or other basis	(e) Basis for depreciation (business/investment use only)	(f) Recovery period	(g) Method/ Convention	(h) Depreciation deduction	(i) Elected section 179 cost
25 Special depreciation allowance for qualified listed property placed in service during the tax year and used more than 50% in a qualified business use. See instructions						25		
26 Property used more than 50% in a qualified business use:								
		%						
		%						
		%						
27 Property used 50% or less in a qualified business use:								
		%				S/L –		
		%				S/L –		
		%				S/L –		
28 Add amounts in column (h), lines 25 through 27. Enter here and on line 21, page 1						28		
29 Add amounts in column (i), line 26. Enter here and on line 7, page 1							29	

Section B—Information on Use of Vehicles

Complete this section for vehicles used by a sole proprietor, partner, or other "more than 5% owner," or related person. If you provided vehicles to your employees, first answer the questions in Section C to see if you meet an exception to completing this section for those vehicles.

	(a) Vehicle 1		(b) Vehicle 2		(c) Vehicle 3		(d) Vehicle 4		(e) Vehicle 5		(f) Vehicle 6	
30 Total business/investment miles driven during the year (**don't** include commuting miles)												
31 Total commuting miles driven during the year												
32 Total other personal (noncommuting) miles driven												
33 Total miles driven during the year. Add lines 30 through 32												
34 Was the vehicle available for personal use during off-duty hours?	Yes	No	Yes	No	Yes	No	Yes	No	Yes	No	Yes	No
35 Was the vehicle used primarily by a more than 5% owner or related person?												
36 Is another vehicle available for personal use?												

Section C—Questions for Employers Who Provide Vehicles for Use by Their Employees

Answer these questions to determine if you meet an exception to completing Section B for vehicles used by employees who **aren't** more than 5% owners or related persons. See instructions.

		Yes	No
37	Do you maintain a written policy statement that prohibits all personal use of vehicles, including commuting, by your employees?		
38	Do you maintain a written policy statement that prohibits personal use of vehicles, except commuting, by your employees? See the instructions for vehicles used by corporate officers, directors, or 1% or more owners		
39	Do you treat all use of vehicles by employees as personal use?		
40	Do you provide more than five vehicles to your employees, obtain information from your employees about the use of the vehicles, and retain the information received?		
41	Do you meet the requirements concerning qualified automobile demonstration use? See instructions		

Note: If your answer to 37, 38, 39, 40, or 41 is "Yes," don't complete Section B for the covered vehicles.

Part VI   **Amortization**

(a) Description of costs	(b) Date amortization begins	(c) Amortizable amount	(d) Code section	(e) Amortization period or percentage	(f) Amortization for this year
42 Amortization of costs that begins during your 2022 tax year (see instructions):					
43 Amortization of costs that began before your 2022 tax year				43	
44 **Total.** Add amounts in column (f). See the instructions for where to report				44	

Form **4562** (2022)

Leasing Expenses and Deductibility

Leasing a vehicle is a popular option for many Uber, Lyft, and limousine drivers. It provides flexibility and allows you to have access to a well-maintained vehicle without the long-term commitment of buying one. But did you know that leasing expenses can also be tax-deductible?

When it comes to leasing expenses, there are a few key factors to consider. First and foremost, you must ensure that the lease is in your name and that you use the vehicle primarily for business purposes. This means that at least 50% of the miles driven should be for Uber, Lyft, or limousine rides. If you meet these criteria, you can deduct a portion of your lease payments as a business expense.

To calculate the deductible amount, you will need to determine the percentage of business use. This can be done by dividing the total number of business miles driven by the total number of miles driven during the lease period. For example, if you drove 10,000 miles during the lease period and 6,000 of those miles were for business purposes, the business use percentage would be 60%.

Once you have the business use percentage, you can apply it to your lease payments to determine the deductible amount. For instance, if your monthly lease payment is $500 and the business use percentage is 60%, you can deduct $300 ($500 x 60%) as a business expense each month.

It's important to note that only the portion of the lease payment that relates to the business use of the vehicle is deductible. Any personal use portion is not eligible for deduction. Additionally, other expenses related to the lease, such as insurance and licensing fees, can also be deducted in proportion to the business use percentage.

To ensure that you have accurate records, it's advisable to keep a mileage log that clearly indicates the purpose of each trip. This will help support your deductions in case of an audit.

By understanding the rules and regulations surrounding leasing expenses, you can maximize your tax deductions as an Uber, Lyft, or limousine driver. Remember to consult with a tax professional or refer to IRS guidelines for specific details related to your situation.

Deductibility of Interest on Car loan payments

One of the major expenses for Uber, Lyft, and limousine drivers is the cost of their vehicles. Many drivers choose to finance their cars through loans, and understanding the deductibility of the interest on these car loan payments can help maximize tax deductions.

The Internal Revenue Service (IRS) allows self-employed individuals, such as Uber drivers, to deduct the interest paid on a car loan if the vehicle is used for business purposes. This means that if you use your car primarily for driving passengers, you can deduct the interest paid on your car loan from your taxable income.

To qualify for this deduction, it is important to keep detailed records of your car's usage. This includes maintaining a logbook that documents the miles driven for business purposes, as well as keeping track of all car loan payment receipts and statements.

It is important to note that if you use your car for both business and personal use, you can only deduct the portion of the interest that corresponds to the percentage of business use. For example, if you use your car 70% of the time for Uber driving and 30% for personal use, you can deduct 70% of the interest paid on your car loan.

Additionally, the IRS requires that you use the actual expense method rather than the standard mileage deduction if you choose to deduct the interest on your car loan. This means that you must track and deduct all the actual costs associated with your vehicle, such as gas, insurance, repairs, and maintenance.

When it comes to deducting the interest on your car loan, it is important to consult with a tax professional or use tax software specifically designed for Uber, Lyft, and limousine drivers. These resources can help ensure that you are accurately tracking and deducting all eligible expenses, including the interest on your car loan payments.

By understanding the deductibility of interest on car loan payments, Uber drivers can maximize their tax deductions and potentially save a significant amount of money during tax season. So be sure to keep detailed records and consult with a tax professional to ensure you are taking full advantage of this deduction.

Chapter 6: Maximizing Tax Deductions in Home Office and Workspace Deductions

Understanding and documenting Home Office and Workspace Deductions

As an Uber, Lyft, or limousine driver, you likely spend a significant amount of time working from your home office or workspace. Did you know that you may be eligible to claim tax deductions for these areas? In this subchapter, we will delve into the intricacies of understanding and documenting home office and workspace deductions, helping you maximize your tax savings.

First and foremost, it's important to understand what qualifies as a home office or workspace. The IRS defines a home office as a specific area in your home that is used exclusively for business purposes. This can include a room or a portion of a room, as long as it is regularly and exclusively used for conducting your rideshare business.

To claim home office deductions, you need to keep accurate records and document your expenses. This includes maintaining detailed records of your home office expenses, such as rent or mortgage payments, utilities, and repairs. You will also need to calculate the square footage of your home office or workspace and determine the percentage of your home that it represents.

Additionally, you can claim deductions for equipment and supplies used in your home office, such as computers, printers, and office furniture. These items must be exclusively used for your rideshare business to be eligible for deductions.

It's crucial to remember that claiming home office deductions can trigger an audit, so it's vital to follow the IRS guidelines carefully. Keep organized records, maintain accurate documentation, and consult with a tax professional if needed.

In this subchapter, we will provide you with practical tips and strategies for maximizing your home office and workspace deductions. We will explore the specific expenses you can claim, explain the documentation requirements, and offer insights on how to avoid common pitfalls.

By understanding and documenting your home office and workspace deductions correctly, you can significantly reduce your tax liability and increase your overall tax savings. Don't miss out on these valuable deductions that you are entitled to as an Uber, Lyft, or limousine driver. With the information provided in this subchapter, you will be well-equipped to navigate the complexities of home office deductions and optimize your tax savings.

Form 8829 explained

As an Uber, Lyft, or limousine driver, understanding the various tax deductions available to you is crucial for maximizing your earnings and minimizing your tax liability. One of the most important forms you need to be familiar with is Form 8829.

Form 8829, also known as the Expenses for Business Use of Your Home, is used to calculate the deduction for business use of your home. As a rideshare driver, your home office serves as the central hub for managing your business operations. This form allows you to deduct a portion of your home expenses, such as rent or mortgage interest, utilities, and insurance, based on the square footage of your home office relative to your total home.

To qualify for the home office deduction, your home office must be used exclusively for your Uber, Lyft, or limousine business activities. It should be your primary place of business, where you conduct administrative tasks, coordinate rides, and manage your finances. Additionally, the space should be used regularly and exclusively for your business.

In order to accurately complete Form 8829, you must gather all relevant documentation related to your home expenses. This includes receipts, utility bills, lease agreements, and any other supporting documents that demonstrate the business use of your home office.

Once you have gathered all the necessary information, you can calculate your home office deduction using either the simplified or regular method. The simplified method allows you to deduct $5 per square foot of your home office, up to a maximum of 300 square feet. The regular method requires more detailed calculations and documentation but may result in a higher deduction.

By properly completing and filing Form 8829, you can maximize your tax deductions for home office and workspace expenses, ultimately reducing your taxable income. This, in turn, can help you save money and increase your overall earnings as an Uber, Lyft, or limousine driver.

An example of Form 8829 is on the next page.

Form **8829**	**Expenses for Business Use of Your Home**	OMB No. 1545-0074
Department of the Treasury Internal Revenue Service	File only with Schedule C (Form 1040). Use a separate Form 8829 for each home you used for business during the year. Go to *www.irs.gov/Form8829* for instructions and the latest information.	**2022** Attachment Sequence No. **176**

Name(s) of proprietor(s) | Your social security number

Part I Part of Your Home Used for Business

1	Area used regularly and exclusively for business, regularly for daycare, or for storage of inventory or product samples (see instructions)	1	
2	Total area of home	2	
3	Divide line 1 by line 2. Enter the result as a percentage	3	%
	For daycare facilities not used exclusively for business, go to line 4. All others, go to line 7.		
4	Multiply days used for daycare during year by hours used per day	4	hr.
5	If you started or stopped using your home for daycare during the year, see instructions; otherwise, enter 8,760	5	hr.
6	Divide line 4 by line 5. Enter the result as a decimal amount	6	.
7	Business percentage. For daycare facilities not used exclusively for business, multiply line 6 by line 3 (enter the result as a percentage). All others, enter the amount from line 3	7	%

Part II Figure Your Allowable Deduction

			(a) Direct expenses	(b) Indirect expenses	
8	Enter the amount from Schedule C, line 29, plus any gain derived from the business use of your home, minus any loss from the trade or business not derived from the business use of your home. See instructions.	8			
	See instructions for columns (a) and (b) before completing lines 9–22.				
9	Casualty losses (see instructions)	9			
10	Deductible mortgage interest (see instructions)	10			
11	Real estate taxes (see instructions)	11			
12	Add lines 9, 10, and 11	12			
13	Multiply line 12, column (b), by line 7	13			
14	Add line 12, column (a), and line 13				14
15	Subtract line 14 from line 8. If zero or less, enter -0-				15
16	Excess mortgage interest (see instructions)	16			
17	Excess real estate taxes (see instructions)	17			
18	Insurance	18			
19	Rent	19			
20	Repairs and maintenance	20			
21	Utilities	21			
22	Other expenses (see instructions)	22			
23	Add lines 16 through 22	23			
24	Multiply line 23, column (b), by line 7	24			
25	Carryover of prior year operating expenses (see instructions)	25			
26	Add line 23, column (a), line 24, and line 25				26
27	Allowable operating expenses. Enter the smaller of line 15 or line 26				27
28	Limit on excess casualty losses and depreciation. Subtract line 27 from line 15				28
29	Excess casualty losses (see instructions)	29			
30	Depreciation of your home from line 42 below	30			
31	Carryover of prior year excess casualty losses and depreciation (see instructions)	31			
32	Add lines 29 through 31				32
33	Allowable excess casualty losses and depreciation. Enter the smaller of line 28 or line 32				33
34	Add lines 14, 27, and 33				34
35	Casualty loss portion, if any, from lines 14 and 33. Carry amount to Form 4684. See instructions				35
36	Allowable expenses for business use of your home. Subtract line 35 from line 34. Enter here and on Schedule C, line 30. If your home was used for more than one business, see instructions				36

Part III Depreciation of Your Home

37	Enter the smaller of your home's adjusted basis or its fair market value. See instructions	37	
38	Value of land included on line 37	38	
39	Basis of building. Subtract line 38 from line 37	39	
40	Business basis of building. Multiply line 39 by line 7	40	
41	Depreciation percentage (see instructions)	41	%
42	Depreciation allowable (see instructions). Multiply line 40 by line 41. Enter here and on line 30 above	42	

Part IV Carryover of Unallowed Expenses to 2023

43	Operating expenses. Subtract line 27 from line 26. If less than zero, enter -0-	43	
44	Excess casualty losses and depreciation. Subtract line 33 from line 32. If less than zero, enter -0-	44	

For Paperwork Reduction Act Notice, see your tax return instructions.   Cat. No. 13232M   Form **8829** (2022)

In the next subchapters, we will delve into other important tax deductions you should be aware of, including vehicle maintenance and repairs, insurance and licensing fees, fuel and transportation costs, mobile phone and internet expenses, parking and toll fees, vehicle depreciation and leasing expenses, advertising and marketing expenses, and vehicle cleaning and detailing expenses. Stay tuned to learn more about how you can maximize your tax deductions and keep more of your hard-earned money in your pocket.

Visual presentation of Form 8829:

Professional Services and subscriptions

As an Uber, Lyft, or limousine driver, you know that maximizing your tax deductions is crucial for your financial success. Below are a few examples of deductible Professional services and subscriptions. If you have any other professional services and subscriptions that are not below, consult with your tax professional to figure out if they can also be deducted;

Professional Services:

1. Tax Preparation Fees:

Any fees paid to tax professionals or accountants to help prepare tax returns specifically for the rideshare business are deductible.

2. Legal and Consultation Fees:

Costs incurred for legal advice or consultations related to the operation or management of the rideshare business can be deductible.

3. Bookkeeping Services:

Fees paid to bookkeepers or accounting services for maintaining records, reconciling accounts, or managing finances for the rideshare business can also be deductible.

Subscriptions:

1. Business Software:

Subscription fees for software or applications directly related to the rideshare business can be deductible. This might include mileage tracking apps, accounting software, navigation tools, or communication platforms used for the business.

2. Professional Memberships:

Membership dues for professional organizations or associations related to the rideshare industry may be deductible if they are for business purposes and help in the driver's professional development or networking.

Chapter 7: Maximizing Tax Deductions - Tips and Strategies for Uber, Lyft, and Limousine Drivers

Proactive Tax Planning for Rideshare Drivers

As an Uber, Lyft, or limousine driver, you are considered a self-employed individual, which means you have the opportunity to maximize your tax deductions and keep more of your hard-earned money. This subchapter will provide you with valuable insights on proactive tax planning strategies specifically tailored to rideshare drivers.

Maximizing tax deductions for rideshare expenses is crucial for minimizing your tax liability. Keep track of all your business-related expenses, such as mileage, toll fees, and parking expenses. These costs can be deducted from your taxable income, resulting in significant savings.

In addition to rideshare expenses, vehicle maintenance and repairs are another area where you can maximize tax deductions. Expenses such as oil changes, tire replacements, and car washes can all be deducted. Be sure to keep detailed records and receipts to validate these deductions.

Insurance and licensing fees are essential expenses for rideshare drivers, and luckily, they are also deductible. Include these costs in your tax deductions to further reduce your taxable income.

Fuel and transportation costs can quickly add up for rideshare drivers. However, by keeping track of your mileage and fuel expenses, you can claim these as deductions. This includes both business and personal use of your vehicle, so be diligent in maintaining accurate records.

As a rideshare driver, your mobile phone and internet expenses are essential to your business operations. These costs can be deducted, so make sure to separate your personal and business-related usage to ensure accurate deductions.

Parking and toll fees are common expenses for rideshare drivers. These costs can be deducted, so keep track of all parking and toll fees incurred during your working hours.

Vehicle depreciation and leasing expenses are significant deductions for rideshare drivers. If you own or lease your vehicle, you can deduct a portion of the depreciation or lease payments. These deductions can result in substantial tax savings, so be sure to document all relevant expenses.

Advertising and marketing expenses are vital for growing your rideshare business. Fortunately, these costs can be deducted, whether it's for online ads, business cards, or promotional materials.

If you have a dedicated home office or workspace for your rideshare business, you may be eligible for a home office deduction. This deduction allows you to deduct a portion of your rent or mortgage, utilities, and maintenance costs.

Lastly, vehicle cleaning and detailing expenses can also be deducted. Keeping your vehicle clean and presentable is crucial for providing a positive experience for your passengers, and these costs can be written off as business expenses.

By understanding and implementing proactive tax planning strategies, you can maximize your tax deductions as a rideshare driver. Be sure to consult with a tax professional to ensure you are taking full advantage of all available deductions and minimizing your tax liability.

Maximizing Deductions through Year-Round Planning

As an Uber, Lyft, or limousine driver, you have the opportunity to maximize your tax deductions and keep more money in your pocket. By implementing year-round planning strategies, you can ensure that you are taking advantage of all the deductions available to you, ultimately minimizing your tax liability. In this subchapter, we will explore various ways in which you can maximize deductions in different areas of your rideshare business.

One key area to focus on is rideshare expenses. Keep track of all your expenses related to driving, such as tolls, parking fees, and even car washes. These costs can quickly add up, and by keeping detailed records, you can deduct them come tax season.

Another important aspect to consider is vehicle maintenance and repairs. Regular vehicle maintenance, such as oil changes and tire rotations, can be deducted as business expenses. Additionally, any repairs necessary to keep your vehicle in good working condition can also be deducted.

Insurance and licensing fees are another area where deductions can be maximized. Make sure to keep records of all your insurance premiums and any fees associated with licensing or permits required for your rideshare business. These expenses are essential to your business operation and can be deducted accordingly.

Fuel and transportation costs are significant expenses for rideshare drivers. Keep track of all your fuel expenses, including receipts from gas stations. Additionally, if you use public transportation or rideshare services for business purposes, those costs can also be deducted.

In today's digital age, mobile phone and internet expenses are inevitable for rideshare drivers. Deducting a portion of your mobile phone bill and internet expenses can result in substantial tax savings. Keep track of your business-related usage to determine the percentage that can be deducted.

Parking and toll fees can quickly add up for rideshare drivers. Keep track of these expenses, as they are deductible. Additionally, if you lease a vehicle, you can deduct a portion of the lease expenses as well as vehicle depreciation.

Advertising and marketing expenses are essential for growing your rideshare business. Deducting costs related to business cards, flyers, online advertising, and even referral incentives can help maximize your deductions.

For those who use a home office or workspace, you may be eligible to deduct a portion of your rent or mortgage, utilities, and even home internet expenses. Keep accurate records of your business-related usage to determine the deductible amount.

Finally, vehicle cleaning and detailing expenses can also be deducted. Regularly cleaning your vehicle is essential for providing a pleasant experience to your passengers, and these costs can be deducted as a business expense.

Maximizing your tax deductions as an Uber, Lyft, or limousine driver requires careful year-round planning and accurate record-keeping. By paying attention to these various areas, you can ensure that you are taking advantage of all the deductions available to you, ultimately minimizing your tax liability and maximizing your income.

Seeking Professional Tax Advice

One of the most important aspects of being a successful Uber, Lyft, or limousine driver is ensuring that you maximize your tax deductions. As an independent contractor, you have the opportunity to deduct various expenses related to your ridesharing business, which can result in significant tax savings. However, navigating the complex tax laws and regulations can be challenging, which is why seeking professional tax advice is crucial.

When it comes to maximizing tax deductions for Uber drivers, there are several key areas to focus on. First and foremost, rideshare expenses are one of the largest deductible categories. This includes commissions paid to Uber or Lyft, booking fees, and any other expenses directly related to your ridesharing activities. A tax professional can help you identify all eligible deductions and ensure that you are claiming them correctly.

Vehicle maintenance and repairs are another significant expense for Uber drivers. From regular oil changes to major repairs, these costs can quickly add up. A tax expert can guide you on how to properly deduct these expenses, including keeping detailed records and understanding the difference between repairs and improvements.

Insurance and licensing fees are essential for any rideshare driver. These expenses are generally deductible, but it's crucial to understand the specific rules and limitations. A tax professional can help you navigate the complexities of deducting these costs and ensure that you are maximizing your deductions.

Fuel and transportation costs are another area where Uber drivers can save on taxes. Whether it's gas expenses, public transportation fees, or parking fees, these expenses can be deducted, but it's essential to keep accurate records and understand the specific requirements.

In today's digital age, mobile phone and internet expenses are often necessary for rideshare drivers. These costs can also be deducted, but it's crucial to understand the rules surrounding personal versus business use. Seeking professional tax advice can help you ensure that you are claiming these deductions correctly.

Other areas where professional tax advice can be beneficial include parking and toll fees, vehicle depreciation and leasing expenses, advertising and marketing expenses, home office and workspace deductions, and vehicle cleaning and detailing expenses. An experienced tax professional can guide you through these deductions and help you maximize your tax savings.

In conclusion, seeking professional tax advice is essential for Uber, Lyft, and limousine drivers looking to maximize their tax deductions. With the help of a tax expert, you can navigate the complex tax laws and regulations, identify all eligible deductions, and ensure that you are claiming them correctly. By doing so, you can significantly reduce your tax liability and keep more money in your pocket.

Common Mistakes to Avoid

As an Uber, Lyft, or limousine driver, you have the opportunity to maximize your tax deductions and save money. However, there are several common mistakes that drivers often make when it comes to claiming deductions. By avoiding these mistakes, you can ensure that you are taking full advantage of the tax benefits available to you.

One common mistake that many drivers make is failing to keep accurate records of their rideshare expenses. Keep meticulous records! It is essential to keep detailed records of all your expenses, including gas, maintenance and repairs, insurance and licensing fees, and even parking and toll fees. Without proper documentation, you may not be able to prove your expenses and claim the deductions you are entitled to.

Another mistake to avoid is not fully understanding the rules and regulations surrounding tax deductions for rideshare drivers. For example, many drivers are unaware that they can deduct a portion of their mobile phone and internet expenses if they use them for work-related purposes. By familiarizing yourself with the tax laws specific to rideshare drivers, you can ensure that you are taking advantage of all available deductions.

Mixing Personal and Business expenses is another common mistake we see. Clearly distinguish between expenses used soley for rideshare work and those with personal overlap, like phone usage. Most importantly DO NOT overestimate. Inflating deductions can raise red flags with the IRS and get you boggled down in correspondence (usually mistakenly called an Audit, which is totally different and more detailed.) Be honest and accurate in your reporting.

A common mistake is mixing Personal and Business expenses. Clearly distinguish between expenses used soley for rideshare work and those with personal overlap, like phone usage. Most importantly DO NOT overestimate. Inflating deductions can raise red flags with the IRS and get you boggled down in correspondence (usually mistakenly called an Audit, which is totally different and more detailed.) Be honest and accurate in your reporting.

Another common mistake is overlooking small deductions. Some drivers overlook small expense such as tolls or parking fees, assuming they are not significant. However these small costs add up and fully deductible. For example paying $10 in tolls and parking fees everyday for 330 days is $3,300 that can be deducted from your income.

One area where drivers often miss out on deductions is vehicle depreciation and leasing expenses. It is important to keep track of your vehicle's depreciation over time and understand how it affects your tax deductions. Additionally, if you lease a vehicle for your rideshare business, you may be able to deduct a portion of your lease payments.

Advertising and marketing expenses are another area where drivers often make mistakes. Many drivers are unaware that they can deduct expenses related to promoting their services, such as business cards or online advertising. By keeping track of these expenses and properly documenting them, you can lower your taxable income.

Lastly, drivers often overlook the deductions available for home office and workspace expenses. If you use a portion of your home exclusively for your rideshare business, you may be able to claim a deduction for these expenses. It is important to understand the rules surrounding home office deductions and ensure that you meet all the requirements.

By avoiding these common mistakes and staying informed about the specific tax deductions available to Uber, Lyft, and limousine drivers, you can maximize your savings and keep more money in your pocket. Remember to keep accurate records, educate yourself about the tax laws, and take advantage of all the deductions you are eligible for. With proper planning and attention to detail, you can minimize your tax liability and maximize your tax deductions as a rideshare driver.

Chapter 8: Conclusion and Final Thoughts

Congratulations, rideshare drivers! You have reached the final chapter of "The Ultimate Guide to Maximizing Tax Deductions for Uber Drivers." Throughout this book, we have explored various ways to help you maximize your tax deductions and minimize your tax liability. As we wrap up this journey, let's recap some key takeaways and final thoughts to ensure you make the most of your tax deductions.

Maximize tax deductions for Uber drivers in rideshare expenses:
Remember to keep detailed records of all your rideshare expenses, including commissions and fees paid to the platform. These expenses can significantly reduce your taxable income.

Maximize tax deductions for Uber drivers in vehicle maintenance and repairs:
Regularly maintain and repair your vehicle to ensure it is in optimal condition. Keep track of all maintenance and repair expenses, including oil changes, tire replacements, and repairs. These costs can be deducted from your taxable income.

Maximize tax deductions for Uber drivers in insurance and licensing fees:
Keep copies of your insurance premiums and any licensing fees paid. These expenses are deductible and can help lower your tax liability.

Maximize tax deductions for Uber drivers in fuel and transportation costs:
Track your fuel expenses and other transportation costs, such as parking fees and tolls. These costs can be deducted from your taxable income.

Maximize tax deductions for Uber drivers in mobile phone and internet expenses:
If you use your mobile phone and internet for business purposes, you can

deduct a portion of these expenses. Keep records of your bills to substantiate your deductions.

Maximize tax deductions for Uber drivers in parking and toll fees:
Save all receipts and records of parking fees and tolls paid during your rideshare trips. These expenses are deductible and can significantly reduce your tax liability.

Maximize tax deductions for Uber drivers in vehicle depreciation and leasing expenses:
If you own or lease a vehicle, you can deduct a portion of its depreciation or lease payments. Keep accurate records of your expenses and consult with a tax professional to determine the best method for your situation.

Maximize tax deductions for Uber drivers in advertising and marketing expenses:
If you engage in advertising and marketing activities to promote your rideshare business, these expenses can be deducted. Keep receipts and records of your advertising costs.

Maximize tax deductions for Uber drivers in home office and workspace deductions:
If you have a dedicated home office or workspace, you can deduct a portion of your rent, utilities, and other related expenses. Keep records of your expenses and consult with a tax professional to ensure you meet the necessary criteria.

Maximize tax deductions for Uber drivers in vehicle cleaning and detailing expenses:
Maintaining a clean and presentable vehicle is essential for your rideshare business. Keep records of your cleaning and detailing expenses, as they are deductible.

In conclusion, understanding and maximizing your tax deductions as an Uber, Lyft, or limousine driver can significantly impact your overall tax liability. By keeping detailed records, consulting with a tax professional, and staying up-to-date with tax laws, you can ensure you are taking full advantage of the deductions available to you. Remember, every dollar saved on taxes is a dollar earned for your business. Best of luck in maximizing your tax deductions and achieving financial success in your rideshare endeavors!